Making the Laws:

The Legislative Branch

By
Dr. Latina Campbell

Print ISBN: 978-1-966491-12-5

eBook ISBN: 978-1-966491-13-2

Printed in the United States of America

Story Corner Publishing & Consulting, Inc.

Chesapeake, VA 23321

Storycornerpublishing@yahoo.com

www.StoryCornerPublishing.com

Dedication

I dedicate this book to all the children who dream of becoming the future president, members of Congress, judges, lawyers, politicians, law enforcement, or even military. Be fair and just with everyone and do everything in love and kindness. Put God first and allow Him to lead you through every decision.

In the meantime, remember no matter who holds office or what laws are passed, God has the final say and remains in control. There's no need to worry about things you see happen in the world, just pray to God. Prayer changes everything.

P.S.

I'm proud of you because you are brave!

Do you ever wonder how laws are made,

Or who decides what can be obeyed?

In the United States, there's a special team,

Called the Legislative Branch—it's like a dream!

This branch is part of the government three,

It works with the others in harmony.

The Legislative Branch writes laws, you see,

To keep us safe, fair, and free!

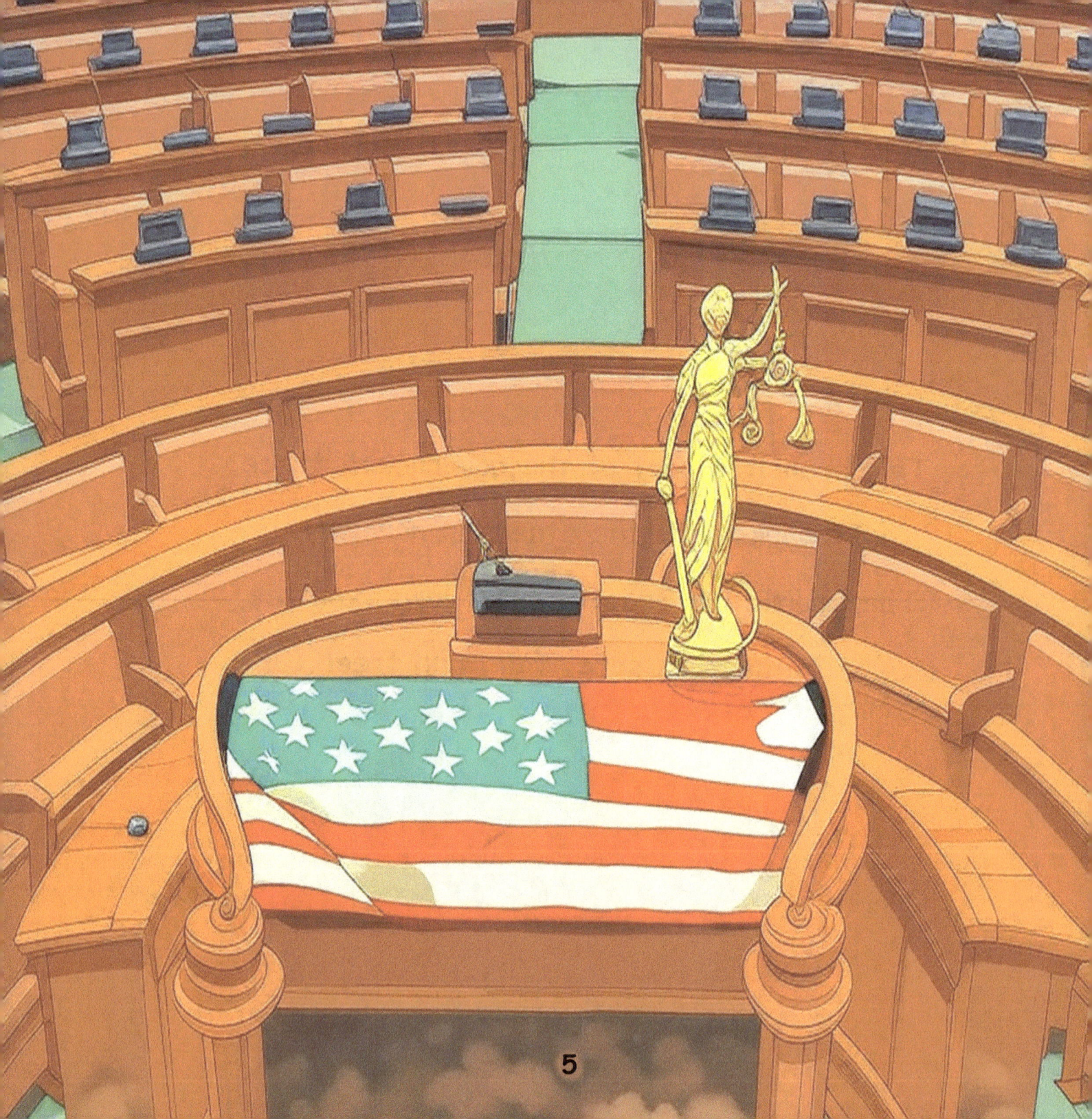

The Legislative Branch has a special name,

It's called Congress, with important fame.

But what is Congress? What do they do?

Let's take a closer look—it's fun to pursue!

Congress has two parts, both big and strong,

Working together to get things along.

One is the Senate, wise and steady,

The other's the House, busy and ready!

The Senate has two people per state,

No matter how big or small their fate.

From California to Rhode Island's shore,

Every state gets two—no less, no more!

11

The House of Representatives is the other side,

With numbers based on each state's size.

Big states like Texas get many to share,

While smaller states send just a few there.

The people we elect to these two groups,

Are called lawmakers—what a troop!

They work for us, they hear our needs,

Then write new laws for important deeds.

15

But making a law isn't quick or fast,

It's a process that has to last.

A law starts as an idea, simple and small,

Then it's written as a bill, and that's not all!

The bill gets discussed, debated, and read,

In both the Senate and House, it's said.

If they vote "yes," it's passed along,

To the President, to see if it belongs.

The President can say "yes" with a sign,

And the bill becomes a law in time!

But if the President says, "No, not yet,"

Congress can vote again—don't forget!

The Legislative Branch does more than write laws,

They listen to people and their cause.

They approve budgets and money to spend,

On schools, roads, and help to lend.

They also make sure that leaders are fair,

Checking the government everywhere.

The Legislative Branch is strong and wise,

It works for the people—it's no surprise!

So now you know about Congress today,

And how it helps in every way.

The Legislative Branch makes laws we obey,

To keep our country strong each day!

The next time you see a law that's new,

Think of Congress and all they do.

Working together, big and small,

To make a better world for us all!

The End

www.ingramcontent.com/pod-product-compliance
Lightning Source LLC
Chambersburg PA
CBHW081542120626
46550CB00009B/2828